DATE DUE

JUN 0 4 2005		

Demco

Portraits
from an
Unfinished Woman

Portraits
from an
Unfinished Woman

Ruth
Swaner

Covenant Communications, Inc.
American Fork, Utah

Thanks, Louise,
for your continual support,
and always, your love.

Library of Congress Catalog Number 90-086124
Covenant Communications, Inc.
Portraits From an Unfinished Woman
Printed May 1991
ISBN 1-55503-316-4

Dedication

To my best friend, my mother,
Who taught me through her example,
Who is in everything I do ,
Who is part of me,

and

To my husband, Roger,
a gentle, quiet man,
who always keeps me on track.
And to those wonderful boys—
my four sons,
Shawn, Derrick, David, Michael.

Contents

You would know the secret of death.
But how shall you find it unless
you seek in the heart of Life?

—Kahlil Gibran

Your joy is your sorrow unmasked.
The deeper that sorrow carves
into your being, the more joy
you can contain. When you are
joyous, look deep into your heart
and you shall find it is only that
which has given you sorrow
that is giving you joy.

—Kahlil Gibran

Prologue

*T*his book will confirm my testimony of the importance of documenting one's life. The accounts it contains demonstrate the power of love in action, the victory over daily and lifelong struggles, and the growth received through a refiner's fire. I found that hard work has its rewards, sensitivity to others develops my love, and wisdom comes when I stop looking for it.

I've always had close friends, friends I call my "depthy ones." They're the special beings in my inner circle. Long ago they included my mother, my Grandmother Harris, my neighbor, Hattie, and others.

Today I boast ten or more souls on whom I rely for "depthy" friendships. The buds of my inner circle of friends blossomed where I began—in the town of my birth.

Why have I never moved from this high mountain valley where I was born? I live two blocks east of the location where I grew up—or pretended to grow up—for 17 years before going away to college.

In my childhood home I was secure as an only child, but lonely. Now with Mother and Father gone I've become more insecure in my insecurities. I stepped too early into solitude, trying to find truth in nature, music, painting, and often friendships. I knew I was ignorant pretending to be wise, lazy pretending to work hard, and over-sensitive to what others thought of me. Truth, I find is not neatly contained in a package, waiting to be unwrapped.

Portraits, images from my past, burn in my memory. Sometimes I wish I could reach inside to snatch up those tender scenes with loved ones and live them once again.

The truth I found then, and now, remains as portraits cherished by an unfinished woman. And when I become whole and complete, the real truth will still be remembered in the sweetness of their faces.

My Nanny

Yes, I had a nanny. My parents weren't rich. We didn't live in a big estate circled by a black wrought iron fence. A limousine and a swimming pool were not part of our wealth. But I had my nanny. Her name was Isabell Crockett.

Smithfield, Utah, I suppose, is an unlikely place to find nannies for hire. I don't know if Isabell got paid or not, but in those days money was hard to come by. My two grandmothers lived with us, and Mother and Dad both had jobs outside our home.

Isabell lived across the street. While I was still snuggled in my bed dreaming tomgirl dreams, she arrived at our modest home each weekday morning. Breakfast was served, dishes were done and my two grandmothers were given their cups of tea to sip them awake.

Isabell, with deep brown eyes and short-cropped curls, shook me awake with, "Time to get up, lazybones. Hurry—your oatmeal will get cold."

She was a familiar face, but she wasn't the face I longed for. I wanted Mother to kiss me awake but she was already waiting on customers at the J.C. Penney store in Logan.

Isabell had a dry sense of humor. Her mouth always seemed ready to burst into a smile, but it never did. My parents loved her. I loved her too.

As I entertained my two grandmothers with circus acts and daring shows of strength, Isabell rolled dough, made pies, swept floors and ironed. I often recall the sight of steam rolling up from the ironing board and remember hearing that "clomp, clomp" noise. Isabell would slam the hot iron down just in the right place to make the wrinkles disappear from Dad's white shirts. She also smoothed beds into snuggly nests, beckoning me for afternoon naps.

As I awakened from those naps with a familiar stuffed animal under my arm and a favorite patchwork quilt nestled under my chin, my nose led me to the kitchen. Isabell would just be taking two lemon meringue pies from the oven. The meringue on top was the work of a craftsman. It crowned the lemon with white golden fluffs. The chiffon peaks were kissed with a tinge of sunny brown. What a pleasant way to wake from a nap! To this day I can see, smell, and taste Isabell's mouth-watering pies.

She was a peacemaker when my two grandmothers each wanted the same section from the newspaper. Isabell also became the referee when they wanted to watch television. Grandmother Harris chose to watch the prize fights. Grandmother Thorpe wanted the Lawrence Welk Show. Isabell settled the disputes with diplomacy and kindness.

Isabell was a caregiver. Grandmother firmly believed that the only way to start out the morning was to rinse each eye with water. Isabell routinely filled Grandmother Harris's special eyeglass with lukewarm water. The container was the size and shape of an eyeball and would hold the warm water right on each eye as she blinked the sleep away.

But most of all Isabell was my friend. She bandaged cuts, washed out knee wounds, and she taught me about bugs and insects. She told me witchy stories and explained to me why rainbows are arched. Whether she was right or not didn't matter to me. She was there and answered all my endless questions.

The world of creativity was offered to me by Isabell. On poster paper I was allowed to cut, glue, draw and paste to my heart's content.

She was a kind woman filled with wisdom and quick solutions to problems. I'll never forget the day I found out there really wasn't a Santa Claus. I said, "Isie, there isn't a Santa Claus. My friend told me he isn't real."

Her dark eyes gleaming, she cupped my face in rough hands and whispered, "Don't tell your parents. They don't know yet."

What wisdom and insight her answer carried for me years later when I really understood.

One humorous memory of Nanny Isabell is connected with a cold winter's evening.

Mother and Dad decided to go out to dinner and a movie. They could hardly back out of the driveway. Snow flurries swirled under the glimmering street lamps. Dad roared up the motor and plowed backwards through the snowbank and into the street.

As I pressed my nose against the frosty window, I saw Isabell hobbling across the street and up the steps into our house.

My two grandmothers sat in Boston rockers, teetering back and forth in unison.

Isabell and I shook popcorn awake over flaming logs in the fireplace. The inhabitants of our cozy room soon grew sleepy. Grandmother Harris snored between each knitted stitch of her handiwork.

The wind howled around the house and the storm outside blew and grew in intensity. I crept closer to the fire.

Isabell kept looking at her watch. She beckoned me to her side and held me close. Bedtime soon became the necessity of the moment. I was tucked into my stuffed animal haven first. My grandmothers' frail bodies welcomed their beds an hour later.

I was asleep and unaware of Isabell's dilemma the rest of that evening. The story was told to me the following day.

Isabell washed the dishes, straightened the newspapers, and sat watching the last hot embers disappear beneath the grill in the fire pit. By then it was 11 p.m. Isabell, knowing we were all asleep, decided to put on her coat and go across the ice-covered road to her home. She wanted to make sure everything was all right there.

While she was gone, Mother and Dad pulled into the driveway, parked the car in the garage and shut the doors. When they went inside everyone was in bed and Isabell could not be found. Thinking that she had gone home for the evening, my parents went upstairs to bed.

Isabell, only away for five minutes, returned to our home. She settled into a comfortable chair and began tatting. She was an artist at tatting beautiful ruffles on handkerchiefs.

As the hour drew closer to midnight, Isabell's concern for my parents magnified. Thinking they may have been stuck in the snow or hurt in an accident, she wondered what course of action to take.

At 1:30 a.m. Isabell could wait no longer. She first called the neighbors and asked everyone to join in the search along snowy roads in hopes of finding my parents if they were stranded. Then the police were called.

At 3 a.m. our living room was filled with concerned neighbors and the police. Isabell paced the floor, pausing only to look out the window now and again.

My parents, safe in their beds upstairs, were suddenly awakened by the activities in the living room. Dad slipped on his bathrobe and Mom followed him down the stairs. Thinking there were burglars in the house, Dad grabbed his shotgun from the gun rack. Mother carried an old broom she had found in the hallway.

Halfway down the stairs, my parents peeked into the partially opened door of the living room. Recognizing their friends and neighbors, Dad dropped his gun and gazed over the crowd. Mother hid the broom behind her back. Isabell turned white. Looking at my parents, she stuttered: "Where did you come from?"

After both sides of the story were told, everyone had a good laugh. In our neighborhood that experience was the topic of every conversation for some time. Isabell pledged never to leave our home again, even for a few minutes, unless she left a note to let someone know of her whereabouts.

Isabell's love and concern for my parents, exemplified by that wintry evening, was reflected throughout her life in service to our family.

Several years after that incident, neighbors were again assembled in our living room. It was another cold winter evening, and I was eight years old. All of us were waiting for the phone call we didn't want to answer. I sat close to the fireplace and recalled all those times that Isabell and I had roasted chestnuts, popped corn and talked of wonderful things. The phone rang, and the room grew silent. Dad answered the call. His mouth turned downward as he listened intently. "Yes, yes, I'll tell them. Thank you. Goodbye."

Dad walked over to me and sat on the floor; his huge arms encircled my young shoulders. "Ruth," he said, "that was Isabell's brother calling from the hospital. Isabell just died."

I looked into the fire and felt I wanted to be engulfed by the flames. Instead, I held onto Dad and cried.

Later that night after everyone had gone to bed, I sneaked downstairs, unable to sleep. As I sat in my grandmother's rocking chair I looked into the black, cold fireplace. For hours, silence filled my aching heart, then through the stillness, a warm feeling wrapped me like a cozy blanket. I realized Isabell hadn't left me at all. She was a part of me—the way I looked at things, my creativity, my love of life and lemon meringue pies. Isabell had instilled in me a thirst for adventure and a close kinship with nature through her lessons about the wonders of the world. These things I will always have. Her legacy has been instilled in me.

Isabell's old wooden-framed house stood west of the church. Now nothing is left of her home. A parking lot covers any traces of her existence. Smithfield Creek is the only thing that remains; that stream where I used to soak bare feet on hot summer afternoons. I remember her whenever I see it.

I am forever thankful for sweet friends such as Isabell, whose lives have blended with mine. I realize that they have deeply influenced who I am and who I want to become . I am not alone, however, in discontent with "being," for it is, instead, in the eternal process of "becoming" that the greatest Friend of all divinely guides us.

The Locket

*A*s I was growing up, an only child, my best friends were my grandmothers who lived with our family until their deaths.

One week before my Grandmother Harris died she summoned me to her bedroom. Grandmother was always a familiar sight, rocking in her Boston rocker, her purple shawl wrapped around her lean shoulders and her familiar hearing aid hooked to the front of her dress with the earplugs nestled in both ears.

I kissed her and knelt by her side. "Ruth," she said, "I'm going to die soon and when I do, everyone will come in here and start grabbing things and hauling them off. Go over to the dresser and bring me that blue velvet box."

I went to the dresser, returned with the box and placed it in her wrinkled hands. She opened it and gently pulled out a beautiful gold locket. It displayed a white diamond in the center with emerald-colored sequins surrounding it. Inside was a picture of her and Grandfather when they were married.

She put the locket in the case and instructed, "Now remember, when I die, you come into my room and take the locket. It's yours. I want you to have it."

I sighed, "Grandmother, you're not going to die." Then I saw the earnest look in her eyes and affirmed, "But I'll remember."

One week later, the night before she died, my father called me to Grandmother's room. "Kiss your grandmother goodbye. She may not be here tomorrow," he said soberly.

My feelings were ambiguous. At age ten I was too full of life to understand death. I declared, "I'll kiss her goodnight but NOT goodbye."

The next morning I rushed downstairs as usual, thinking of my plans with Grandmother today. When I ran to her room, the scene I encountered was indelibly impressed on my mind.

I looked at her bed. There were clean sheets and pillow cases, with not a sign of a wrinkle. Cold, clean, sterile sheets and white folded-down covers. Uninhabited. Suddenly empty, like my heart.

Father came into the room and put his arms around me and stammered, "Your grandmother is gone."

"Gone where?" I demanded.

"She died last night," he cried, and left me to my thoughts and confused feelings.

I couldn't believe it. My constant house companion for over ten years—gone! I didn't know what to do. Then I remembered Grandmother's words, "Go to the dresser. The locket is yours."

I turned to the dresser, retrieved the blue box and stumbled upstairs, throwing myself on the bed. I clutched the blue velvet case next to my heart. When I opened it the locket fell into my hands. Tears streamed down my face, and for some time I gave into the fullness of mourning.

Embracing the locket I finally realized that this object was my living gift from Grandmother and that through the locket she would still be my constant companion.

Years later as I was about to be married in the Logan Temple, the feeling of Grandmother's presence confirmed her love for me.

Other brides and I, all dressed in long white wedding dresses, sat in a circle in the Brides Room. While speaking to us about eternal marriage, President Raymond's wife suddenly paused and looking down at me revealed, "Sister Harris, I feel compelled to tell you at this time that your special Grandmother Harris is with you today and will be by your side throughout the ceremony."

I knew it was true. I lovingly, tearfully fingered the locket around my neck.

How choice it is to have *experienced* the truth that we will all live again. We *will* greet those who have passed away before. Yes, I will hug my beloved grandmother again, see her face, and share in her goodness—and then it will be for the eternities!

The Departure

A crowd had gathered at the Cache Junction train depot early that spring morning. I still remember the feel and sound of feet walking across the boardwalks.

Relatives and friends, after hugging each other, got on the rickety old train. Its destination was every jerk-water town from Cache Junction, Utah, to Portland, Oregon.

I reflected back at what it must have been like when families kissed their sons goodbye as they boarded trains heading for combat and the unknowns of World War II.

This spring day in 1964 was a less intense scene but still an experience which takes its place in my heart.

Dad and I had said goodbye to Mother at this station numerous times before. As a small child I had sometimes gone with her. The destination was always the same: Portland, Oregon, to see my brother and his family.

I wouldn't be going on this trip, however. At age eighteen I was departing on new adventures. My departure time was not known and my time of arrival was even more uncertain.

I had just graduated from high school, and faced major decisions which would influence the rest of my life. It was a frightening position for me. Had I really changed from an ugly duckling tomgirl into a confident young lady?

Mother kissed Dad goodbye and gave me a hug. She grabbed the railing with one gloved hand and held onto her hat with her other hand. A cold breeze blew through the station as we watched her make her way through the crowded aisle to her seat.

I gazed at Mother's beautiful face framed by the window as she lovingly peered out at us. Her delicate features and penetrating blue eyes pressed upon my heart. The stately hat and fur collar silhouetted her radiant face.

Her life as my mother passed instantly before my eyes. She had accomplished so much. Would I be as courageous and filled with as much love as she had been? Would I give as much? She had given not only to her family, but to her church and community also. Her countenance displayed a woman with strength, ability, and most of all, a woman with confidence.

In contrast, I remembered my growing up years, especially the awkward stages of junior high and early high school years. I was tall and thin, and my bad complexion was all I could see of my youthful face. I hated the image I saw in the mirror.

At the school dances I was always the last one to be asked. The pain I felt at those occasions was sometimes more than I could bear.

Did Mother ever hate herself, I wondered. At eighteen was she ever frightened for the future, wanting to forget the past?

I blew her a kiss and put my arm around Dad. Part of him was seated in that train, too.

It seemed like an eternity as I looked at Mother with her face pressed up against the window. For a moment my eyes were distracted by someone else. Sitting in the seat in front of her was a young girl with her finger pointing directly at me. Her countenance displayed an unfamiliar look of admiration.

Just at that moment she turned and said something to her mother sitting next to her. Overhearing the little girl's words, my mother stood up, made her way down the aisle, and got off the train.

She walked over to me with misty eyes and held me close. "Do you want to know what that little girl said?" Mother asked.

"Yes, I guess so," I said reluctantly.

Mother pressed her cheek against mine and whispered, "That sweet little girl said to her mother, 'Look Mom, look at that pretty lady. I want to look just like her when I grow up!'"

I was shocked and overwhelmed. The pride in my mother's eyes shone in agreement.

The uncertainty about myself and the future was silenced that morning by the momentary look of admiration from a little girl's face and by the power of a mother's tender love.

Hattie

She stood by the splintered door with those outlandish laced army boots on her feet and her faded red-flowered apron flapping in the wind. Her earth-brown hair was cropped short and the tangled curls lay in a mass around her face. But eager blue eyes fixed on me.

Hattie was like her house—old and shabby but homey and inviting and still standing with pride. I was only a child the first time I saw her. Other kids were afraid. They made fun of her, but I sensed even then how alone and sad she was.

In the same way the ivy had crept across the windows and roof of her old log house, lines had mapped their course on her face, erasing a long-ago youth. Her leathery skin, once soft, now told the story of her life.

"Come in child, come in. I've just baked some sugar cookies." The aroma teased my nose. Inside her cozy one-room cabin, wallpaper had once been bright but now was faded—at least where it showed between

Hattie's growing display of Christmas greetings, birthday cards, and yellowed newspaper clippings.

Every day I went to Hattie's, spending summer afternoons eating cookies, watching her take fresh-baked bread out of the big black oven, and listening to wild tales of past adventures.

She wasn't sad as I had originally thought. She was just tired. Her life was the past more than the present and now it was time to turn back the pages and reminisce.

I heard stories of tired and courageous women who toiled in wartime factories making weapons and the tanks which ultimately rumbled down cobbled streets and liberated Paris.

She showed me her hands scarred where hot metal had scorched her fingers and calloused from past and present tribulations.

Hattie taught me that if you don't have a passion for something in life and make the passion work within you, then life isn't worth living. "You must care about something so strongly that you put your love into action," she advised. "Love is no good without action."

As Hattie placed her hands on my shoulders, she declared, "Love life but use your trials to your advantage. Grow, and pass on what you have learned."

All through my youth I visited Hattie. Even after I went away to college I always tried to visit her on weekends and holidays.

Her passion for life had sparked an answering passion in me. That zest for living helped me learn and share. Because of Hattie, I wasn't afraid to love or care about people or causes. I met a young man who felt as I did and together we grew, still searching for what Hattie already had. The pure essence of life for Hattie was: love self, love others, and love God.

Hattie's life had been filled with poverty and hard work. But in spite of her lack of material things, she always seemed to have love to give away. She gave me something more important then sugar cookies and apple turnovers. She gave me "Hattie."

The day I told her I was going to be married, she took my soft small hands in her big rough ones and we shared tears of joy.

Then it was the day before the wedding ceremony. Hattie summoned me to her house. She pointed to my wedding announcement pasted on her wall scrapbook as if it were a prized trophy. Hattie went to the old dresser, pulled the top drawer open and retrieved a small white box.

"I want you to have this. It's all I have. I haven't much money. This was my mother's."

She gently placed it in my hands. With a broken voice she said, "You've been like a daughter to me."

I was stunned and touched by her words. My hands shook as I opened the box. Lying in a nest of cotton was a heart-shaped brooch which glittered in the sun streaming in from her broken window. It looked as if it were worth about a million dollars in that golden light. It was worth more than that to me in love.

"Hattie, it's beautiful. But . . . but are you sure you want me to have it?"

Her sunken gray eyes filled with tears and an affirmative nod answered my question. I hugged her frail body and suddenly realized how weak and aged she'd grown.

I didn't go to see Hattie after that day until two years later when I slowly walked up her weedy path, five months pregnant. The brooch I wore on my blouse shone in the sun as brightly as the day I first saw it.

The house was quiet. It seemed to lean to one side. The cedar logs and windows were completely hidden by the evergreens. The door was the only thing showing among the woody stems and forest of vines.

I knocked faintly at first. Then I pounded on the door that had opened so many times to welcome me with warmth and sugar cookies. No answer.

Finally, I walked away, defeated by silence. Just as I approached my car a neighbor called out to me, "Are you looking for Hattie?"

"Yes, yes I am," I said.

Then all the times Hattie had comforted and taught me crowded my mind as I heard, "I'm sorry to be the one to tell you. Hattie died today."

I clutched the brooch and the words seemed to echo in my ears as I thought of visits unmade, time unshared.

"Love is no good without action," the echo repeated again and again.

That day I recommitted myself to make visits, share my love, take some form of action before it's too late. If I don't move upon my feelings of love, what good is loving? I must give it away, share it.

Hattie died today, but the loving ways she taught me will never die.

Thaya, the Editor, and Thaya, the Woman

*S*he didn't appear as I imagined an editor should look. She stood almost six feet tall. Her long brown hair fell limply over her shoulders. Her only features which calmed me were her subtle blue eyes and gentle voice.

Thaya, my editor, asked me to tag along on an interview. As I watched her pull out tender answers from a hesitant woman, I was amazed at her talent for interviewing.

Driving back to the office we passed the nearly-constructed hospital. To my surprise, Thaya veered the car to the edge of the road and stopped. "Well, Ruth," she said sternly, "You've been complaining enough about getting better stories. There's your story." She pointed to the hospital. "I heard that they're hiring small-framed college girls to climb into the ceilings of the rooms to put up insulation. Go interview them." She handed me a pad and a pencil.

I stayed up all night finishing the story. Stacks of paper littered my home office. All I could hear was Thaya as she dropped me off at my home: "I want it on my desk tomorrow morning." Where was that gentle, soft voice, I wondered.

The finished copy was placed on her desk while she was out to lunch—very good planning on my part. The next day it appeared on the second to last page of the paper. The heading read: "Three girls make big money in small places."

I heard a joke going around the office, circulated by Thaya, that if she had a nickel for every misspelled word in Ruth's article she would be a rich woman.

I left her office five years later to work for a larger newspaper. Looking back at my training, I realized that Thaya was not only patient but long-suffering in her faith in me. Abundant in experience and molded by Thaya's stern but caring hands, I can say, "I never made her rich."

Yet it wasn't until four years after I had been hired by the other newspaper, I realized that behind all of Thaya's teasing, firmness, and occasional coolness towards me, was a woman with tender feelings.

I was a patient in the Logan Regional Hospital. On the fourth day of my recuperation after the unplanned surgery, I felt different. I cried, mourning a loss, a death, a taking away of something I had carried since birth. My surgery had been a result of a ruptured tubal pregnancy. Half of my reproductive system was removed. My right ovary and tube were gone, one potential baby gone!

I buried my head in my white hospital sheets, crying silently. Unable to sleep, I tossed and turned. I finally slipped on my robe and slippers and opened the door. It was almost midnight. The nurse was sitting at her station with her back turned. I noticed a large empty room at the end of the hall. As I walked inside, my eyes caught a warm glimmer of light coming from the window. The Logan Temple with its towering majestic pinnacles peered through at me. Gratefully, tearfully, I remembered my wedding day.

I stood for a long time at the window feeling both thankful and sad, sad because I didn't feel like a complete woman. Even though it wasn't like losing a breast, I still felt sorrow. As tears easily came, I felt hands on my shoulders. I turned to see Thaya looking at me with love-filled eyes. "I was just going home from working late in the office and something told me to drop by and see how you were doing," she said.

As we sat alone in the dark room I recounted every detail of the last four days.

The conversation was not about writing or editorial deadlines, but about a loss, a woman's sorrow.

Thaya reached out and held my hands and quietly confirmed my feelings, "I know, Ruth, I do understand. I had my right tube and ovary removed two years ago. It was also a tubal pregnancy."

I suddenly realized that Thaya's promptings to see me that night came from a higher source.

Years later I found my journal entry for this experience. At the end of the page I have written: "Thank you, Thaya, for understanding those feelings which are totally and uniquely a woman's. And God bless all women who risk to share, who reach out with compassion and love, who help the rest of us feel less alone in our losses."

A Loving Intervention

I felt spiritually numb. I could neither listen to the counsel of others nor assimilate their advice into my life. I felt smothered with church responsibilities, my children's endless requests, and a husband whose job demanded most of his time and energy.

With bits and pieces of me being snatched by the demands of family, church, and friends I felt broken and unfulfilled.

I also suffered from low self-esteem. I believed that the Lord did not care about me, that he didn't love me. If my own family, with whom I lived hourly, were not aware of my needs, how could Heavenly Father be aware? He seemed so far away.

As my visiting teachers arrived for their monthly visit I put on my usual "happy face." I hid the torment I felt inside. We exchanged trivial happenings in our lives. I felt invisible as their words glided past me.

As we stood at the door saying our good-byes, I thought, what a waste of time.

They don't realize how I feel inside. Even if they did, would they care?

I mechanically worked through my routine chores. My body wanted to retreat to sleep. I was surprised when the doorbell rang. I wasn't expecting anyone.

As I slowly opened the door, Julie, one of my visiting teachers, stepped inside. She took my hands in hers and asked, "Ruth, do you have a quiet room in your home where we won't be disturbed?"

Not understanding her question, I replied, "Julie, why are you here again?"

She said lovingly, "When I returned home today I couldn't get you out of my mind. When we visited earlier I saw the anguish in your eyes. Everything I did today seemed meaningless. Finally I stopped my work and knelt in prayer. I asked over and over again, 'Lord, help me to help Ruth.' I realized the answer was not totally in my asking the words, but in what I was doing, physically kneeling down before my Heavenly Father."

I stood in silence through Julie's explanation. With tears filling her eyes she affirmed, "Ruth, I felt compelled by the Spirit to come back today. I know you are having trouble praying and I know you don't feel loved by your Heavenly Father." Her words seized me. I could not deny the truthfulness of her discovery. "Is there a room where we could be alone?" she asked again.

"Yes, I guess so . . . my bedroom upstairs," I stammered.

As we stood by my bed she said, "Ruth, I'm going to pray first, then I want you to pray."

I interrupted, "Oh no, not me! I don't want to ask anything anymore."

Julie pulled me to my knees as she knelt beside me. "I love you, Ruth, and so does Heavenly Father," she said.

"Just ask him this one simple question: 'Do you love me, Heavenly Father?'"

Julie prayed. Her special prayer in my behalf softened my heart. The sweet spirit filling the room subdued my anger and frustrations. I realized that Heavenly Father was near and he was waiting.

At the conclusion of Julie's prayer she reached over and took my trembling hands in hers. "Now it's your turn, Ruth."

A long silence blanketed the room. Finally the words came. "Heavenly Father, do you love me?" Tears flowed freely as I asked again, earnestly.

Within moments my answer was received in the silence of my heart. "You need not ask what you already know." The answer was repeated, "You need not ask what you already know."

The words were given with warmth and love. As I received them I pondered all the times I had known Heavenly Father was near, showing his love for me. Now this instant I was invited to feel of his eternal love once again. Suddenly I knew for sure—His love had been there all along.

Care Package Child

*Y*ou could call her by her professional name—clinical psychologist, or head coordinator for handicapped services. But I called her "friend." She was someone who helped me to find, accept, and love that little girl inside of me.

I first met Phyllis when she and a team of college graduates evaluated my son. That's when the nightmare became a reality. Yes, my son Michael was retarded. Yes, he was autistic. "But, he looks all right!" I demanded. "He looks normal. He's not physically deformed. Just look at him," I cried. After giving birth to three healthy sons, I couldn't accept the possibility that Michael wasn't just as normal.

Weeks had spilled into months of rejecting the fact that Michael was retarded. Not accepting kept me from enrolling him in the special school where Phyllis was the clinical psychologist.

I remember Phyllis then, on our first

meeting. Her eyes had compassion and love for me even at our first visit.

My journey began in April. I searched the closet for the perfect dress. I showered and shampooed my hair. I tried to act cheerful as I put on my bright red lip'stick—just normal, happy Ruth. But by the time I arrived at the school alone that day, my mood had changed. Feelings of terror swelled within me.

I sat in Phyllis's office looking out at the green, rain-soaked lawn. The sky was gray and heavy. So was my heart.

Phyllis placed her hand on my shoulder. I was startled by her touch. I bolted upright, grabbing the arms of the chair.

"Deep in thought?" she asked.

"Yes, I . . . I guess so," I stuttered.

"Tell me, why are you here? Are you ready to enroll Michael in school?" she questioned.

"No. Yes. I don't know. I just can't seem to accept that he is really retarded. I like to be in control of things," I admitted.

"Are you out of control?" Phyllis asked.

My eyes fixed on the window. I didn't see the approaching storm or the swirl of leaves blowing across the campus. I only saw the reflection of my face. Why was that question so hard to answer? Or was it? I pondered. I stared at the brown tweed carpet, hoping she wouldn't see the tears, or my hands twisting the tissue in my lap.

"I feel so alone. . .frightened," I whispered.

"What did you say, Ruth?,"

"I think I want to be held," I said, surprised that I could verbalize my feelings. Phyllis left her side of the desk and pulled up a chair next to me. Her arms encompassed me. Burying my head into her shoulder, I cried. Then I pulled back, wiped my tears and stated matter of factly, "I'm a grown woman. I'm an adult. I shouldn't do this. I'm not a child."

Phyllis looked at me, studying my face. "You know, Ruth, we are all children at times. Each of us has three parts to ourselves," she explained. "We are the adult, the nurturing parent, and the child, all wrapped into one. It's all right to want to be held and nurtured like a child at times."

We both agreed that first afternoon that I needed therapy; help not only in accepting that Michael was not normal, but also in accepting and loving myself.

On the third visit Phyllis asked me to bring a picture of myself as a child. I found a picture I hated—a picture of a little girl in a knitted pink dress. She had big blue eyes with lips that turned down at the corners. It was a sad face, the look of a care-package child. A child with no home, no family, nothing. I didn't wear tattered clothes, but my face was the face of a lonely, lost child.

"Why do you hate this picture so much?" Phyllis asked.

I squirmed in my chair. It would take weeks for her to pry out the reasons.

As an only child born to older parents, I was lonely. My best friends were my two grandmothers who lived with us. Through deeper counseling, a picture of my mother's influence became clearer. She was always doing compassionate service or working with some committee. Consequently, I got off the school bus every day and returned home to a house void of a mother.

I'd been a spoiled child who always got what she wanted by throwing tantrums. Now as an adult I wanted to control every circumstance of my life. Having a retarded child was not in my plans.

During the following months of therapy, the deep hidden feelings of loneliness, of feeling unloved, and the hunger for physical attention instead of material gifts, gradually surfaced. From role-playing to tearing up magazines to vent my anger, Phyllis lovingly persisted in making me stretch and search for the real Ruth. Instead of dealing with accepting my son as not normal, she concentrated on my accepting "me" as an adult, a child, and a nurturing parent. Some of the confrontations with her had made me angry. Sometimes I ran from her office or yelled at her. In the beginning when we role-played, I laughed at its potential importance in helping me. Even though I couldn't see that I had changed and grown, Phyllis could. I figured on this October day there would be no new surprises. I was wrong. As I sat in her office I remember how I'd squirmed that first day sitting in this chair and how frightened I was. Phyllis had brought me full circle.

Phyllis walked into the room carrying a white folder. She closed the door, and we exchanged greetings and chit chat. Then she asked me to bring over the rocking chair which was sitting in the corner of the room.

Putting the rocking chair next to her, I sat in it. Phyllis slid the unopened folder close to me.

"Ruth, you have been coming here every week for the past six months. In the beginning you fought against feeling the hidden pain deep within you. But you have taken that inward journey. You have been courageous in seeing yourself, forgiving others for their infringements upon you and for their lack of love. And, you have almost accepted that care package child inside, but not quite," Phyllis advised.

She opened up the white folder. The picture of me at six years old—the care package child with big sad eyes jumped up at me.

"Here, take it," Phyllis demanded. "Pick it up!"

"Why?" I asked. "You know I hate that picture of myself."

Phyllis pulled her chair closer to mine.

"Your last big role-playing part is today, Ruth. I want you to detach yourself from this picture, Phyllis instructed. Pretend that the picture isn't really you as a child. Pretend that she is 'your' child."

Phyllis leaned closer.

"If this were your child how would you treat her? What would you say to her?"

I let her questions bounce off me. I didn't want to play this part. I didn't want to love that little girl in the picture. I didn't know how.

"Tear down the last brick wall," Phyllis encouraged. "Feel Ruth, really feel. Feel until it hurts." I sat motionless in the rocking chair. I stared at the picture in my lap. Painful silence filled the room. Phyllis waited. I waited. Then after what seemed to be a full day pushed into a few moments, suddenly I realized I was rocking back and forth in the rocking chair. I held the picture close to my breast.

"What do you feel for this child, Ruth?" Phyllis whispered.

The room became blurred as tears filled my eyes. I leaned my head on the back of the chair and looked at the ceiling.

"I love her and I'd hold her," I cried.

"Tell her," Phyllis exclaimed.

I looked at the picture with a mother's love. "I love you. I love you," I sobbed and kissed the picture. "You're a beautiful girl. You are loved and always will be. I'm going to take good care of you," I found myself saying.

Phyllis held both of my hands and declared, "Look at me, Ruth, this picture is yourself as a child. You can love her. You can love yourself. You can hold her and accept her. You can take care of her. This is you, Ruth."

Phyllis wiped her eyes, then handed me a tissue. "And when you can love and accept yourself, you can love and accept your retarded child."

I threw my arms tightly around Phyllis. That instant awakening, the rebirth of Ruth that day was a turning point. My journey was finished. I knew my therapy was at an end. The struggle was over. On that crimson autumn afternoon I became a friend to myself, loving that little girl inside.

Taking Care of Michael

*M*arch 17, 1982 (Journal Entry) . . .

Michael's teacher taught me what to look for when he has petit mal seizures. I saw several today. His eyes drift off. Sometimes his head drops down and he loses his balance.

He's on a drug now. Hope it works. It tastes terrible. We have to hold his arms and legs and shove it down his throat while one of us holds his nose. I hate it. It drains me every night to go through this ritual.

March 19, 1982

Michael's new medication has turned him into a four-and-a-half-year-old monster. A violent rage is coming out from his little body. He scratches and kicks me. It takes me 30 minutes to get him dressed every morning. I can't take much more of this. The doctor says the phenobarbital has caused a personality change. How could my beautiful angelic child turn into such an angry beast?

March 30, 1982

Michael has become completely obsessed with water and dirt, climbing, bouncing up and down, and continually rocking.

We put all our potted plants out of reach so Michael can't take the dirt out of them. We also had to put outside locks on all of the bathroom doors because he was continually playing in the toilets, showers and sinks. I can't stand to live this way. Lord, please help me.

May 13, 1982

I can't believe Michael will be 5 years old tomorrow. In some ways I have dreaded this day. I always thought a miracle would happen and he would catch up on his motor and learning skills by now. He hasn't and he never will. I guess subconsciously I always knew he wouldn't attend public schools, but I wouldn't admit it to myself.

He's becoming more loving towards me, however. He loves to cuddle and hug me, but sometimes he still pushes me away or bites my shoulder when we're hugging. I hope someday his seizures will be under control. I also hope that someday Michael will speak to us. I long for the day when he says "Mother." I guess with all the bad things that have happened to Michael, a lot of good things have happened to the rest of us. Some days I thought I would never make it. But I wake up the next morning still alive and ready to try all over again.

The challenge in coping with my autistic son began in the summer of 1978. Finding out your child is handicapped is one thing. Accepting it is another.

When I was told my 6-month-old son had a "neurological problem" I reacted like most human beings would—with shock.

A physician had noticed the way my child flailed his hands and suggested there might be problems. That was a shocker to even think there was something wrong. That set me on a path leading from denial to acceptance—a path I still retrace occasionally in coping with the problems of my son.

Looking back on the ups and downs I realized that I needed to love myself before I could love and accept Michael. That was the turning point—a realization that I had to explore my own feelings and that I could ask for help. There were some crushing moments to be endured before I reached that point.

The worst day of my life was when my husband and I took our six-month-old Michael to the Primary Children's Hospital in Salt Lake City for testing.

All I can remember is going from one

room to the next for tests. Some nurse would come in and take the baby out of my arms and take him into another room for the test. When Michael returned he was crying and tired. I kept hearing little children crying in other rooms and it started to unnerve me.

By the end of the day when doctors asked my husband and myself to hold the baby's arms while they did a blood test, I'd had enough. I went out to the car and fell apart.

We returned to the hospital a second time to meet with doctors. It was at that meeting the doctors advised us, "Your child has brain damage." They told us that they didn't know how or why the damage had occurred.

I remember the doctors telling us that our child "may possibly be dependent upon us the rest of our lives . . . may never attend public schools . . . and will probably lack good judgment."

The doctors then encouraged us to take Michael to the Exceptional Child Center at Utah State University, praising it as one of the best facilities available.

When we rode home, Roger and I were completely silent. We were in a state of shock. I think disbelief was part of our problem, and a feeling of hope that the doctors were wrong.

It was at least a month before I called the Exceptional Child Center. I just couldn't. I knew if I picked up the phone and asked for help, I would be saying I believed my child wasn't normal.

However, I eventually did call the Child Center and scheduled an evaluation for Michael. He was accepted in the home-bound program and became a student in the autistic class. As a family we had to accept many changes in our day-to-day living. A great deal of time had to be spent routinely teaching Michael basic things like crawling, walking, and feeding himself.

By the time Michael was three-and-a-half, other developmental problems showed up. He didn't talk and therefore couldn't tell us what he needed or how he felt—a great frustration for a mother. Then there was the uncontrollable flailing of the hands which happens when he gets excited.

Looking back, I can identify about ten different emotional stages I went through—some more than once.

One was anger.

An early test at the Child Center convinced even me that Michael was severely deaf along with his other problems.

The anger came out on the way home. He was giggling and having a good time on the seat, but his mother was going through hell. . . . All I wanted to do was scream. I looked up at the sky and asked, "What more is going to happen to my child?"

Later a sophisticated test administered at the Primary Children's Hospital reversed the earlier suspicions and showed that Michael was not deaf after all. He was just not responding to sounds! (This was a symptom, I found out later, of autism.) It made me furious that I had been told he was deaf. I boiled over with the anger of frustration.

I drove to a friend's home after the test. I couldn't speak because I was so angry and so full of emotions I couldn't express. The thing I wanted to do was take my shoes off, go over to the river, throw them in—then jump right in after them.

My head pounded with unanswerable questions: "Why can't someone help him? Why does he have to go through all of this? I don't need or want any of this. Why can't my beloved Michael just be normal?"

Part of my frustration was living in a world of unknowns. Doctors gave me a lot of maybes and ifs, a lot of big words but no certainties. "What do these words mean?" I remember asking myself.

I credit some close friends with helping me through the early days but other well-meaning friends hurt me.

I remember a fellow church member trying to comfort me with thoughts that God had given me a special child. She was well-meaning, but I didn't need that right then. I didn't want a special child. I just wanted a normal one. Viewing my friend's actions now, though, I'd probably have said the same thing to somebody else.

I felt I had to protect myself from what I thought others were saying or thinking. I became very defensive for a time. However, my defensive wall came tumbling down one day when a little six-year-old boy knocked at my door. He blurted, "My mom told me you had a 'retarded' kid. I want to see him!" I felt hurt for an instant, then I realized he was just curious.

I took his hand and walked with him into Michael's room. Michael was resting, "starry-eyed" in his crib. The little boy looked him over from head to toe and quickly replied, "Gee, he doesn't look retarded! He looks just like you or me."

Tears came to my eyes as I gently gave him a hug, "Yes, Johnny, I know."

One of the symptoms of autism is withdrawal by the autistic child into himself. Michael was totally in another world at times, completely unaware of what was happening around him.

Ever since Michael's problems began, guilt was a big problem for me. I think guilt is the worst thing anybody can carry. You've got to feel like a complete person and a responsible person in order to stay on top of things. The word I hate most in the English language is guilt, because guilt leads to discouragement, and discouragement leads to great depression.

But I did go through guilt. One of my first questions to a doctor was whether smelling glue could cause brain damage.

Eight months pregnant, I had purchased a load of carpet squares and glued them to the floor of a room in my home. My fears were that I may have breathed too many of the fumes into my system causing brain damage in my unborn child. My doctor eliminated my concern.

Besides feelings of guilt, I also felt sorrow in the fact that I wouldn't be able to share with Michael what I share with my other children. We are a family that enjoys singing, playing the piano and guitar, and going on long walks and bike rides. During these simple pleasures we talk about wild and wonderful things. It was frustrating to me that I could never fully share these precious experiences with Michael. His silent world was, at that time, impenetrable.

Michael, in the beginning, was always in his dream world. I woke up every morning not knowing what to expect from him.

Since making the decision to accept Michael's condition and learning how to cope with it, I have been active in the program to help my son. I began a study of autism to understand my son's problem better. My family also is taking an active role in Michael's growth. We have been taught how to use sign language using symbols with our hands while actually saying the word, because Michael will communicate through a few simple gestures, but does not speak one word.

I received help from friends, counselor, church and God, but in the long run I was left alone to gain that inward strength to cope with an uncontrollable situation.

Before Michael, I lived a nice, quiet life with only a few minor difficulties. I loved to be in control of every situation. But this situation was one in which I had no choice, no control. I had to and will have to live with this problem as long as I live.

There are going to be days when I go through these stages again. It's not like my son has a cold and is going to get over it. Learning to cope is going to be a lifelong process.

I recognize that there will be days I can't cope. On these days I'll read the scriptures, pray, talk it out with someone, or go to my own private mountain where I can understand from a distance who I am.

I remember the day I tended my neighbor's three-year-old and what an intense delayed reaction I had to that experience. This child was talking, running, communicating in every sense and he was alert to the world around him. He was obviously "normal."

After his mother returned I carried out the routine activities of the day. The next day I woke up extremely depressed. I didn't want to get out of bed. I couldn't figure out what was triggering my depression.

As the day wore on I realized that I was subconsciously comparing Michael to the three-year-old neighbor child. But I could not allow myself to compare Michael to any other child. It wasn't fair to Michael or to myself.

It's sometimes hard, but through my struggles with Michael, I have gained a new sensitivity to the simple joys which come from observing, helping, and loving. A simple smile, a loving hug, and nature in its purest sense . . . these all mean so much to me.

I remember a special moment somewhere in the beginning of the struggle. One moment, one vision which will live in my mind forever. From my daily journal . . .

"The house was quiet. The children were in school, and I was busy in the kitchen. I glanced around the corner of the cabinets and witnessed a beautiful sight. Michael was sitting on the floor in the middle of the music room. The darkness of the day cast a peaceful soft shadow on his angelic face. A glimmer of sunlight suddenly pierced through a cloud. The whitened rays dashed like silver arrows across the room and fell upon Michael's hands. He lifted his beautifully delicate fingers to greet the sun. Repeatedly, he tried to capture the silver rays. On this day I beheld the simple pleasures and sounds of my angel child Michael."

I reflect often on that tender moment. And like all other visions of treasured moments, I cherish it. Whether I reread those experiences from my journal, or whether reflections move in and out of my awareness during a busy day, nothing can take away the blessing of past memories—*all* of them.

"Love Thy Neighbor As Thyself"

*T*hey could have moved anywhere in our beautiful valley, but they moved next door. For over ten years, Janet, her husband, and their seven children have been a part of our lives. We've enjoyed backyard picnics and overnight summer outings. My three older sons often pair off with three of theirs for games and sports. We shared our summer garden harvest. We borrowed sugar, butter, and diapers—all the while knowing we really didn't have to pay them back.

In the beginning, Janet and I shared brief chit-chats over the backyard fence. We pulled weeds along our borders, making a clean tidy line between our yards. And we maintained a tidy neighborliness, always sure to keep our feelings, trials, and deep concerns behind the private walls of our homes. Then one single unorchestrated experience changed our surface friendship into a tender, deep, and nurturing one.

My morning was to be filled with accomplishing all the tasks on my list. I started by straightening the house. Suddenly I glanced at the clock, only to realize that Michael, my autistic son, had missed the bus to his special school. I'd have to drive him, but did I dare leave him even for a moment to go upstairs and get dressed? I'd have to chance it and hope he would be content listening to music on the stereo.

I rushed upstairs to dress—fast, but not fast enough. Coming back downstairs, I sensed a disaster as I opened the living room door, gazed around the room and distantly into the kitchen and bathroom.

Michael had tipped over every potted plant in the house! Dirt was spread over all the furniture, strewn throughout the carpeting and even into the grand piano. If that wasn't enough, he had turned on all the water taps, and finding a cup, had poured water on top of the dirt. His muddy tracks were everywhere and he was a grimy mess.

I could not reprimand him. Michael has no judgment faculties—he doesn't know the difference between right and wrong. I watched him giggling and playing in the mud. Had he been normal, I would have punished him and made him help clean up the mess. But Michael would never understand. The burden was mine—mine alone that day, since my other sons were gone and my husband was at work.

Anger, disappointment, and frustration all gave way to despair. I barely made it back upstairs before I broke with emotion I had been trying to hold back. Throwing myself on the bed, I gave in to my feelings of facing yet another uncontrollable situation with my autistic child. I recalled many similar incidents that had happened before. Why couldn't I deal with it now?

The recent death of my mother left my tears closer to the surface, and the thought of Michael, still on the rampage by himself downstairs, didn't help. I turned on my back and stared at the ceiling, which appeared warped through my haze of tears. Everything seemed muddled and confused. So much for my well-planned day.

From the floor beneath me, I heard a crash, followed by muffled laughter. It was more than I could take. I reached for the telephone. Three times I dialed trying to reach my closest friends, but none of them were home. A fourth friend said she couldn't come for an hour, but asked if there was someone else she could call to help me in the meantime, perhaps a neighbor. My jumbled thoughts somehow focused on Janet. But she was just my "borrowing neighbor." How could I ask her to help me? But she also had a handicapped child. I'd seen Janet wheel Jeri Dawn to the same bus my son took to school. While Jeri Dawn had cerebral palsy, which bound her to a wheelchair, she did have good mental understanding. Michael, in contrast, was mentally damaged, but his motor skills were normal. And those motor skills were wreaking havoc this very instant in my living room. Would Janet be able to translate her trials with her daughter over to mine with Michael? It was worth a try. I gave my friend Janet's number.

Almost before I got off the bed, the doorbell rang. I wiped the running mascara off my cheeks and soberly went downstairs. With intense embarrassment, I opened the door. I couldn't speak. Janet stepped inside and looked over Michael's destruction. Without hesitation, she reached for the telephone to call another neighbor to drive my son to school. Then she took me by the hand and urged me back upstairs to rest and calm down. "I'll take care of your living room," she assured me in a warm, caring voice and left the bedroom before I could respond.

More tears found their way down my face. I hadn't meant to fall apart. I didn't want anyone to see me like this, especially Janet, whom I'd only allowed to share the good times with our family.

I crawled into the center of the bed and curled into a fetal position. I knew this was not how a grownup woman should behave, but I felt useless. Why was it so difficult for me to admit I had lost control? Why did I feel guilty for turning my problems over to someone else? I shivered—I was cold and weighed down with depression. I wanted to sleep it all away.

I awoke an hour later with a splitting headache. I ignored the pain and dashed downstairs. My eyes followed the edges of the room. All my plants had been repotted, the carpets vacuumed, and even the piano had been cleaned and polished from every trace of dirt, inside and out. I couldn't believe my eyes! Or my nose. On the cabinet was a freshly-baked loaf of bread. A card had been placed nearby. "We have a common bond," it read, "and not just with our children. I understand how you feel, for I have also ached for a friend to fill my drained cup. I am your neighbor. I want to help you. Please let me. Janet."

From that day on, the phrase "Love thy neighbor as thyself" brought more meaning to my life. Janet could have moved almost anywhere in our lovely valley, but the Lord sent her next door. For over ten years we have helped each other with daily tests, with our handicapped children, and with refilling each other's cups.

". . . for better is a neighbor that is near than a brother far off." Proverbs 27:10

A Moment Too Late

I rushed breathlessly to the elevator. It seemed like an eternity before I reached the third floor. The March winds blew with resounding fury outside the tall windows of the hospital. I felt a deep, empty spot in my heart. My hands were cold and shaking.

The exploratory surgery was over. Mother would be resting, unaware of the outcome. Why my mother? Why now? She needed to spend her remaining years doing whatever she wanted to do—vacationing, reading, or just being home.

The elevator stopped abruptly on the third floor. The thought of seeing mother made me cringe. I knew the verdict—cancer. What a terrifying word. The doors of the elevator flew open. I must be strong, strong for her.

The third floor was bustling with visitors, nurses, and children. The spectacle became a haze when my eyes caught for a moment someone sedentary, motionless, a woman alone, sitting in the corner of the waiting room.

This sight would not have caught my attention except that the woman was slumped slightly forward. Her hands supported her face wet with tears. She was alone. People glanced at her only to move on in their tasks.

I was drawn to her, not only because she seemed to be about my age, but because I sensed a strong prompting to go, sit beside her and say, "Can I help? I care."

For one brief instant my legs and heart would have taken me there. But the worldly social pressure of "what would people think" heightened my already insecure feelings. Mother is waiting. I'd better go, I thought. I passed her with great reluctance.

I hurried down the hall, turning left into another hallway filled with more nurses. I must not think about her. I don't even know her. She'd think I was crazy. You just don't do those things.

I reached room 314. Mother was lying still, eyes closed—such a pale, sunken face. Her hair seemed to be whiter than usual. I held her hand. It was cold and unresponsive. "Mother, I'm here." She didn't acknowledge my presence. How long would she be in her medicated state?

Suddenly I realized that I had time, time to do as my heart and spirit had suggested all along. Go back to the woman. She needs you. For some strange reason I care about her. Is it because I, too, am sad and feel helpless in an uncontrollable situation?

I thought of the story of the Good Samaritan. Did he pass by not looking or helping the one in need? Did he worry about what people would think of his actions?

I sprang to my feet. I ran down the hall. My heart pounded in my throat. My mind planned the words I would say to her. I was determined to let my soul and spirit be my guide.

I turned down the busy hall where elevators loaded and unloaded a constant stream of visitors. I stopped, my eyes searching the spot where I last saw her. The chair was empty. I slowly approached the seat. She was gone. Where? I thought. She can't be gone. I needed to give to her. She *was* here. The arms of the chair were still moist with tears. I stood there for a moment with glimpses of what might have been, then slowly I walked back to room 314.

I will always remember that scene: the whisperings of the Spirit, and the heeding of those promptings, too late. In the Doctrine and Covenants 11:12, I read, "And now, verily, verily, I say unto thee, put your trust in that Spirit which leadeth to do good."

There will be other mornings. And with complete dependence upon the Lord there will be a time to listen, to care, to seize the opportunity at hand. Galatians 6:10 reminds me, "As we have therefore opportunity, let us do good unto all men."

The Last Gift

$\mathcal{M}$ade of glass and shiny brass, the miniature music box plays the tune "Memories." This replica of an old record player rests securely in my hands. Memories moisten my face. Like the tune, last Christmas will always be a warm memory.

Mother lived a block down the street. My four sons delighted in stopping there after school for cookies and ice cream. But in December 1981 our lives changed. The traditional feast with the sound of music and the smell of the fireplace burning dry cedar would not be experienced. Relatives couldn't come to mother's house that Christmas.

Mother, sick from chemotherapy, stayed in bed most of December. Her big living room, which traditionally displayed the spirit of Christmas, was bare.

Mother loved Christmas sales. Every year after the holiday she would buy half-price items from the store: trinkets for the tree, wreaths, red-and-green tablecloths, and

Santas of every description. Those boxes held years of holiday sales. She could never throw anything away if it was for Christmas.

But this Christmas Mother tried to keep her pain silent by burying her head in her pillow. The Christmas boxes lay waiting in the basement. She grew worse during the holidays. Still she bravely tolerated her extreme discomfort and even managed to smile when my four sons and I visited her.

Entering my childhood home was a trial of a different sort for me. It was two weeks before Christmas, but the house lacked any sign of it. No Christmas tree sat in the familiar corner by the bookcase. The wreath hook on the front door stood out like a "vacancy" sign asking for something to be hung on it.

I returned home saddened, wanting to have those old traditional Christmases back again. I had to do something to make Mother's home, and maybe her last Christmas with us, a memorable one.

Early the next morning our family purchased a small Christmas tree. It smelled like a blue spruce forest and would look just right in Mother's living room. For an extra dollar we chose pine boughs for her fireplace mantel.

Later that evening when we knew Mother would be resting, the children and I crept into the house. We each had our assigned task. Two boys tiptoed down the basement stairs to get the boxes of Christmas decorations. My other sons helped me put up the tree and assemble the pine boughs across the mantel.

Within two hours we had silently transformed mother's living room into a Christmas dreamworld. Tiny lights blinked on and off through the pine boughs on the mantel. The Christmas tree took its rightful place in the corner reflecting reds and greens on the walls. Sitting on each branch were several small ornaments, tiny houses, and little Christmas elves with cupid faces.

Under the tree I placed a gold tinfoil package which contained the music box. The big pine cone wreath with its delicate blue satin ribbon was hung on the front door.

The sight of the transformed room filled our hearts. We hugged each other, proud of our silent endeavors.

The children couldn't wait to show Grandmother their surprise. We quietly opened her bedroom door. She was awake, and her eyes met ours. We circled her bed.

With eyes as big as Christmas tree ornaments, one grandchild whispered, "Grandma, Grandma, we have a surprise for you in the living room!"

We helped mother through the kitchen and into the living room. I'll never forget the look on her face. The soft glow from the lighted room outlined her head. Tears streamed down her cheeks. With a weak, broken voice she sobbed, "Christmas, Christmas is home again."

Christmas Eve we all gathered in the living room. The lights cast a rainbow of colors on the shadowed walls. In the fireplace, fiery flames danced in rhythm with the Christmas music.

I prepared a turkey dinner with all the trimmings. Mother and my family shared the evening with music, laughter, and warmth. Love filled the room.

Before Mother went to bed we exchanged Christmas presents. I wanted her to open mine first. With shaking hands she slowly opened the box. Frail fingers twisted the key underneath the music box. As we listened to "Memories" our eyes shared a mother-daughter love.

I am awed by the profoundness of those memories. Familiar nights, familiar sounds; all these in a day become memories.

And the future? The future is just waiting to become memories, too.

The Last Gift. Used by permission—*Deseret News.*

The Seed Bed

$\mathcal{A}$s the months of spring melted into shim-
mering summer afternoons, Jane and I
visited mother at the nursing home. Mother
had to have constant medical attention.

Jane was a volunteer worker who helped
our family deal with my mother's terminal
cancer and eventual death. Ironically, I
accepted the fact that Jane wasn't sure there
was a God, and that she perceived death and
the grave as the end. I respected her beliefs
and she respected mine.

We became good friends, yet I silently
questioned how Jane could do volunteer
work helping those of us who would soon
lose loved ones to death. At least I knew I
would see my mother again and that our
family would be together forever. I soon felt
comfortable enough around Jane to share my
faith in God and knowledge of eternal life.
She was polite, but unconvinced.

As mother became worse, my sleepless
nights turned into continual tears. Prayers

offered in her behalf soon turned to pleading with the Lord to take her out of suffering to that peaceful place in immortality.

During these hard times, Jane's love for me was always there, unconditionally. I realized that I was allowing a stranger into my life. I was sharing the most intimate intense, personal experience one could share with another—the death of a loved one.

During those six months of Jane's visits, Mother's affection for Jane blossomed. As she entered Mother's room, they exchanged hugs and kisses. She was like a second daughter. Daily my love for Jane grew stronger as well. She became dear to my heart, like the sister I never had.

The knowledge that Jane was a nonbeliever seemed to fade into obscurity. I loved and accepted her as she was. However, early in August, one week before Mother died, seeds of love and faith planted during all our association with her grew and changed Jane's perceptions of life and death.

I had been strong for such a long time. Each day as I entered Mother's room, I instantly became the parent nurturing the helpless child-mother. I accepted that responsibility with all the strength I could muster.

But that tranquil summer morning was different. I could barely put one foot in front of the other to get to Mother's room. I was drained. I couldn't look at that cancerous, frail body alone today. I called Jane. She arrived and together we walked into Mother's room.

Mother had been so brave and courageous. She still was. Her spirit had been refined and tested. Her sweet countenance and angelic face glowed, overshadowing the deterioration of her diseased body. Seeing and knowing these things became instantly overwhelming to me. At that moment she became, once again, the parent. And I became the child. I embraced her and cried. Her feeble arms held me close and she comforted me through her pain.

I remember her words, "Don't cry, Ruth. Don't be afraid. Everything is going to be all right. Remember, we know we will see each other again. I'll be waiting for you with open arms."

For more than an hour Mother and I talked about dear eternal things. She promised me that when she arrived in heaven she would say hello and give my love to my grandmothers, to my nanny, Isabell, to Hattie, to Sam and Ireta Hymas who had been special neighbors, and also to Harriet Noble, the wonderful old lady who had lived down the street from us. As my emotions of death were replaced with a calm peaceful reassurance of the eternal plan, Mother and I had forgotten that Jane was sitting at the foot of the bed. I looked at Jane and tears were streaming down her face. Mother stretched forth her hands, "Jane," Mother said, "why are you crying?"

Jane sobbed, "My father died when I was three years old. Do you think you could look him up and say hello for me?"

Mother held her close and replied, "I'm sure I'll meet him and I will send your love and message to him."

Mother cupped Jane's face with her wrinkled hands and said, "You know, Jane, you're going to be in heaven with us also. I'll be waiting for you, too."

Love filled the room that August morning; love for one another made meaningful through our sure belief in a life after death.

The seed that had been planted in Jane's heart early in our relationship had taken root. Now the meaning of a scripture filled my mind. "It must needs be that this is a good seed, or that the word is good, for it beginneth to enlarge my soul; yea, it beginneth to enlighten my understanding, yea, it beginneth to be delicious to me." (Alma 32:27.)

The Anatomy of a Death

March 9, 1981 (Journal entry) . . .

Mother went into the operating room at 11 a.m. and it's now 2 p.m. Why so long?

Mother is 75 years old. Her health has drastically deteriorated this past year, especially in the past two months. She's lost so much weight and she's pale. Her hair is white and thin.

Since I've brought her to the hospital I haven't slept much. She may die. Worse than dying, she may continue to suffer.

When I was a little girl I never thought my parents would die. It is all so terribly unreal. I can't sleep now and so I go downstairs and sit in the rocking chair. As I rock I automatically think of my childhood and reminisce about all the good times my mother and I had together. I cry a little and then go to bed.

(Later that afternoon . . .) The operation is over. Mother is back in her room. Her hands are cold. She's still heavily sedated.

(Later that evening . . .) Three doctors surround me in the hallway. These are their comments: "Your mother's kidney has stopped functioning. We inserted a tube in it to help the passageway stay clear." Another doctor: "There is a mass obstructing the entrance of the kidney. It is also surrounding the hip bone and is ingrained in the tissue. We can't remove that part." Third doctor: "You need to take her for an evaluation for possible radiation therapy."

All the time they were talking, they only mentioned cancer once. I wanted to scream. No one would tell me the answer to my question, "Will mother die from this disease?" I guess I knew the answer but I wanted someone else to confirm my fears.

March 15, 1981

After many agonizing days dealing with unanswered questions, I was ready to give up when Carol called. A friend of mine had called her. She is the Director of Hospice of Cache Valley in Northern Utah, a program which provides supportive care for terminally ill patients and their families.

By the time I reached her office I was tight and angry and certainly didn't want to be put off again. I have feelings too. Someone I love is very sick and I can't make her better.

Carol talked with me. She answered all my questions honestly. She weighed her answers carefully but told me the truth to the best of her ability. She had cancer herself and knew the medical terminology. She was a nurse and also had access to Mother's medical records. After several visits with her, I realized I had some hard accepting to do and many decisions to make.

The highlight of that first visit came at the end of our conversation. I turned to her and said, "Carol, is my mother going to die from all of this?"

She replied, "Ruth, we're all going to die sooner or later. From what I know about your mother's case, yes, she probably will. But when, we don't know."

I cried on the way to the car, not because of her comment, but because someone was finally truthful with me and valued my feelings enough to lay it on the line.

(Note: Ten months passed before my next entry. I live near my mother's home. After my husband goes to work and my four sons are in school I pick up Mother for her radiation treatments. Every day we drive 60 miles for the treatments. She had 32 radiation treatments that summer. We also went on numerous trips to local doctors as well as doctors in Ogden and Salt Lake City. The side effects from the radiation treatments started to show up during the last half of the treatments.)

Jan. 25, 1982

I feel numb. The lingering in familiar and unfamiliar waiting rooms has instilled in me an immunity to the sounds of the piped-in music and nurses, always in white (white is worse than black) and to doctors who don't look at you directly.

All I see today is my mother's beautiful face as she hobbles with her cane down the hall, and then rests her frail structure in yet another examination room. I always go with her to give her moral support and to answer questions she can't answer. Daughters always take care of their aging parents, don't they? I'm asked to give them the same information over and over again. It will be added to an already bulging folder.

Today Mother's face and appearance have become almost angelic in nature. There's a sweetness and a quiet glow surrounding her. Her hair has turned snowy white and she's lost so much weight that her skin sags and clings to her bones. Her clothes drown her emaciated form.

A spasm runs its course through my body as I tell this doctor that (according to another physician) a second tumor has been discovered in Mother's neck.

I keep thinking, why doesn't the cancer take her quickly? Why does it have to linger and tease, giving false hopes then suddenly pounding home the reality of the disease. Always, always there is its insidious progression. Is there a reason for all of this?

In spite of it all, I still can't get over the change in Mother. The look in her eyes, the mysterious smile, the heavenly aura emanating from her.

She doesn't talk to me about her cancer or the possibility of her death. What is death anyway except a birth into something more beautiful and lovelier than here and now? But I know and she knows it's serious, and the cancer is there.

I'll miss you, Mother, but I won't miss seeing your pain and suffering and operations. Still I'm glad I'm by your side through your struggles. I'm finding out just who I am, and some day when this refiner's fire is all over, I'll be as crystal clear as the look in your eyes today.

Jan. 30, 1982
I visited Mother today. We talked. It was surfacy. I didn't need any confirmation of how she felt. I could see in her eyes that worried distant look. She had finished a

baby blanket for a close relative. "There, I'm finished with it," she said, almost reluctantly. As she fingered the pink and white blanket, her head tilted to one side, I knew what she was thinking. It was written all over her face: "Will I ever see my new grandchild wrapped in this?"

I find myself wanting to cry with her, but she and I are a lot alike. We're both trying to be strong for each other. Mother, how I love you. Let's be weak together and human; then we can cry together.

Feb. 1, 1982

The reality of knowing I'm soon going to lose my mother strikes me like a bolt of lightning. Little things bring it on, thinking of special experiences and memories. They stir my heart and my pulse quickens. Today my brother called. We talked about funeral arrangements and Mother's personal effects. Why now? She's got us all fooled. She is going to live several more years, isn't she? Dear God, give me the strength to get through this experience.

So much has been left unsaid and undone. I need you so much, Mother, and my children need you. Please don't leave me now.

Today I mentioned to her that she should list on a paper all of her personal possessions and to whom she wants them left. (This was suggested by Hospice.) A Notary Public could sign it making it official.

I had a hard time asking her to do it. She had a hard time accepting the request. She said, "I know I should do it but it makes me feel strange." Just another example that drove home the reality of it all.

Feb. 22, 1982

This was a very hard day for me. A day I will never forget.

I could no longer give Mother the 24-hour-a-day care she needed. Even with all the help from church members, friends, Carol, and the Hospice lay-volunteers, it was still tiring, stressful, and just plain difficult. I have a young family and they also need me.

My half-brothers and I weighed the alternatives, and with the counseling of a few close friends and the Hospice people, we helped mother decide, but the final decision was hers. We knew she wanted to join Dad in the nursing home.

(Our beloved father who had had a stroke and was ailing from emphysema, was already a resident of the nursing home. He had been under specialized medical care for four years. Before my mother became ill, we visited Dad often. He was fourteen years older than

Mother so we assumed our 90-year-old father would die first. Little did we realize that Mother would only be with him at the nursing home for a short time, and she would be the first to leave.)

Fortunately, Mother's name had been on the waiting list, and when a bed became available at the nursing home, Mother decided to take it. The day I picked her up, it was hard leaving Mother's home knowing she might never return. We both took one long look back as I helped her into the car and tears streamed down our faces. My heart sank wondering if we were doing the right thing.

I had to go back to her home during that same day to pick up some things. As I entered that empty house, I cried. Every room had a memory. Every smell, color and sound jarred my heart and pulled at me.

There's the fireplace, the music and television room and the pool room—reminding me of the parties, and the kitchen with its distant memory smells of Christmas meals and Thanksgiving feasts.

I walked through the rooms and they were cold and empty; yet I could still hear Mother playing the piano or vacuuming or singing as she worked.

Dear God, how can I pass this house and

not go in? How can my children remember NOT to stop at Grandma's after school for cookies and milk? How can I lock up my heart and memories as I lock up this empty house where I laughed, cried, studied, shared, loved, and lost loved ones ?

March 8, 1982

Tomorrow it will have been a year since we started these trials, since that first operation and the first numbing bolt of fear that struck my heart as we heard the news a year ago.

A whirlwind of emotions consumed me. As in a nightmare I wanted to wake up from it all. Sometimes I wanted to yell, "Stop! This really isn't happening."

There were special moments, however— scenes so tender and sweet that I find it hard to put them into words. The memories are of Dad and Mother at the nursing home. Dad's room was on Wing Two. Mother had to be placed on Wing Three in Intensive Care.

Every day my dedicated father, clutching his cane in his feeble hand, would slowly hobble down the hall to Mother's room. Many times I witnessed a tender sight. As I peeked into her room, I would see Dad sitting close to Mother, holding her hand. He would sing to her all those wonderful old songs. It reminded me of the evenings at home, when we all gathered around the piano as Mother played and we all sang together.

I also couldn't have made it this far without an understanding husband and the help of the Hospice people. They were there when I needed them. The volunteers were like sisters to me, letting me talk it out, covering the same ground over and over again, rehashing memories, fearful of the next step.

Today my brother and I took care of the funeral arrangements and wrote the obituary. (Another suggestion from Hospice.) Now all we can do is wait, hope, (never give up hope!) pray, and, most of all, spend priceless time with Mother.

Even though the outcome is inevitable, I know that along the way and even for some time after, my Hospice friends will be there. They are like the place called a "Hostel," a place of retreat and rest. They rest me from my cares and give me the strength to go on.

August 8, 1982

What a wonderful two days. I'm now up in the mountains with Shawn, my 11-year-old son. We've made a beautiful campsite, complete with cooking area, tent, ropes between trees to hang things, and much more.

My other three younger sons are taking a two day break with my mother-in-law.

It rained a little last night but we didn't care. We cooked wonderful meals and are now preparing to go on a short hike.

I have thought about writing something extraordinary while I'm up here but no such inspiration has come; I'm too busy being in awe of God's earth.

I thought of this place that has rested me from my worries for a short time. Last night, however, while nestled in my sleeping bag, my heart and thoughts zoomed down this canyon to the valley where Mother lies slowly dying. Oh, how I will miss her when she is gone—I do love her so. Because of her circumstances I feel growing pains and a new era beginning. I guess I'm growing up and growing older. Having these experiences has made me think of what's important in life and what I thought was really important. My heart is filled with love for my dear children, husband, friends, and parents.

August 15, 1982

Mother died yesterday morning at 9:15 a.m. My heart had felt like it had been weighed down with rocks for several days. When I heard this news it was like half the rocks had been removed. A sense of relief came over me, even though sadness and pain were still a part of my feelings.

As I got in my car and drove to the nursing home, I looked up at the mountains where just last weekend I had spent such an enjoyable time with my son.

Somehow I wanted to remember this day, a death day. I wanted to feel and experience everything. I noticed the birds flying in the sky, and the clouds, and the heaven above the clouds. At one point instead of crying I was shouting with joy, "Thank you, Lord. Mother, you've made it! You've made it to a better place. No more pain or suffering."

I arrived at the nursing home thirty minutes after my brother called me. My friend, my father, and my half-brother had already said their good-byes. I entered the room and they left me alone with her. So many days I had sat by her side, held her hand, and stroked her hair . . . so many, many times before.

In early spring I had sat looking out the same window, gazing at the same tree, just budding forth with new leaves. In summer I held Mother's hand as robins nested in the green leaves of that summer tree. The earth stood still there. Outside her window, life was forever taking on more shapes and forms; living, going on into new seasons.

With a shaking voice I said my last good-bye but Mother was above me somewhere (at least her spirit was). I touched that hand and forehead that were once warm. I suddenly felt the coldness—a deathly cold.

When I said my good-byes, that experience was the hardest point thus far in my life. The scene was touching, tense, sad—yet joyous. I'll never forget that moment when I said farewell to my mother. How long we had struggled together and yet how sudden and final that last step—one moment alive, next moment dead.

As I left the nursing home, my body welcomed the light of the early morning sun. The rays covered me like a warm blanket as I walked back down that familiar path toward my car, and on with my life—never to be the same.

Thirty Minutes Before Eternity

8:00 a.m., May 24, 1986 . . .

I brush back the hair from his forehead. He was such a proud man, always proclaiming that his thick head of hair was still dark, even though he was ninety-three.

Releasing my hand from his, I stand up to gaze over old pictures hanging on the walls of his room at the nursing home. I smile and my heart quickens as I gather in my favorite pictures of Mom and Dad proudly standing next to me as I model my university graduation robe and my hat with the tassel.

8:07 a.m. . . . .

Observing his breaths in and out, and in again, fewer and farther apart, I whisper in his ear, "Dad, you're almost home. You're almost home." It seems like just yesterday my four sons were yelling in his semi-deaf ears, telling him jokes and all about their scouting campouts.

8:15 a.m. . . .

He sleeps deeper. The wind outside his window churns up leaves in swirls. They dance out from gutters and coil down the street.

Special memories circle in and out of my mind . . . vacations, fly fishing, picnics in the canyon, trips to Oregon, and yes, the Yellowstone Park adventure.

I look at Dad now, touching his feverish, moist forehead and I think of how he must have been as a young man. His was a hard life. He always declared, "I became a man in Park Valley." That was a lonely time for a fourteen-year-old. When the struggle of clearing sagebrush and herding cattle became unbearable he would sit on the roof of the old log cabin and play his trumpet. The melodious music echoed off the Sawtooth Mountains, blanketing the vast desert of cedar. Music flows through me from several years ago when his crippled fingers played the piano as he sang with his magnificent voice , "The Mother-in-law Song," "Preacher and the Bear," and "Jonah and the Whale."

8:18 a.m. . . .

Ready and willing to die, he sleeps, breathing even deeper. A nurse comes in and observes, "It's almost over." I squeeze his hand a little tighter and speak softly in ears that I know hear me, "You're almost home." I wait in reverent solitude.

He told me just last Sunday, in one fleeting moment, "I love you and you just don't know how much."

I replied, "I love you too, Dad."

I gather up all the tender moments of long, carefree days. They were once faded and a haze, cluttered in the attic of my mind. Now they become instantly cherished.

An "only child" was born to you and Mom. Now, as patience draws thin and love throbs, I realize how much you wanted me and loved me.

8:20 a.m. . . .

Burning tears stream down from my swollen eyes. I find myself saying out loud, "Dad, thank you for giving me the opportunity to come to earth. Thank you for conveying some of your talents to me. Thank you for teaching me to appreciate music, art, good books, and your favorites . . . the fertile earth, nature, flowers, gardens, and animals.

"How I remember 'Pal,' our black Labrador. You certainly taught him fantastic tricks. The day he was killed you were on a trip in Oregon. I called to tell you and we cried together.

"Dear Dad, you were always good for a dollar or two. And I remember how you always wanted me to take you to town to buy Mom a birthday or Christmas present."

8:23 a.m. . . .

I lean back in my chair, stretching my arms out wide. As the reality of this death scene takes hold of me, I wrap my arms tightly around my shoulders and chest, feeling, wishing Mother were here to hold me.

As I give into mourning, my eyes scan his nightstand. There's the bottle of Old Spice aftershave my children gave him last Christmas. It still sits in the corner next to the stacks of old Christmas cards. Next to the large-print Reader's Digest sits a picture of Michael, our youngest. Just last week you said of our retarded child, "I pray for him every night."

8:25 a.m. . . .

Dad's image becomes blurred with my tears. I lean over the bed and kiss his cheek. Sensing an urgency I again whisper,"You're almost home, Dad. Your journey is almost over. When you see Mother again tell her I love her. Give her a hug for me."

The realization that his departure is soon to take place causes words to fall quickly from my mouth, "Thank you for my memories, for your love, Dad. I am *me* because of you and because of the knowledge I have."

As I pick up his hair brush, I put it close to my nose. It smells of him, bringing back memories of each Sunday when I would brush his hair. Now as I brush his hair one last time, a feeling of other loved ones in the room humbles me. Perhaps my mother and others have come to help him home. In reverence to his visitors, I leave to phone his earthly relatives.

8:30 a.m. . . .

I walk back into his room, a room of silence. I sense a journey has ended. Slowly I walk to his bedside. Standing over him I realize he is but an empty shell. Dad's visitors have taken him away. I lean over and whisper one last time, "You made it, Dad. You're home. You're home."

Old Trees Bear Fruit

I wrote a poem once. The last stanza reads . . .

> Precious older ones
> Who, like old trees still bearing fruit
> Have gifts to give
> But no one to give them to.

For five years, my four sons and I traveled to the nursing home each Sunday to visit my father. The trembling hands of the elderly were always extended to us as we walked down the halls. As we shared ourselves with my father, our love gradually grew to include many of the other residents.

First of all there was Thelma and her roommate, Millie, who lived across the hall. Thelma was a retired French professor. She had never married. Without a husband, children, or living relatives (except for one brother), she lived in a lonely world, forgotten. But during those five years of visits, my 15-year-old son learned to speak a little French and was more prepared for his first French class in high school.

Holding hands was easy for me to do. I held Millie's hands, as she told me about how it was years ago in the valley . . . no cars, no plumbing, no electricity. She described her hardships in childbirth, the deaths of four children, and harrowing winters. I would always leave her room counting my blessings for modern conveniences, hospitals and warm rooms on chilly nights.

My father also remembered his difficult past. But even at age 93, he was young in thought, witty, musical, and friendly. There were many men like my father, giving and sharing with those who would stop long enough to listen.

In the lounge, my eyes gathered in old women creating fine stitchery with twisted fingers. Hanna, a Swedish woman, was one of them. She would proudly show me her delicate tatting which transformed an ordinary white handkerchief into a work of art.

Then there was Colleen. Like many time-worn women with the mothering instinct still in them, she clutched a rag doll. She was retarded and one leg was shorter than the other, and the image of her limping down the hall will always linger in my memory.

With one hand she pushed a cart filled with Montgomery Ward catalogs. With the other hand she carried, ever so tenderly, her worn-out rag doll. Every time we met she would motion for me to pick up a catalog. I would thumb through it until she pointed to her favorite page, the doll section. "Baby, baby," she proclaimed as she looked up at me.

Precious older ones, who, like old trees are still bearing fruit. I didn't realize how precious until last May when Father died. Saddened by my loss, I could hardly bring myself to go to the nursing home the next day to remove his belongings. To enter his room and have him not be there was more then I could comprehend. But in order to get the painful experience behind me, I arrived early the next day.

As I tearfully placed his books and clothing in boxes, I felt a hand on my shoulder. Colleen gently placed her rag doll in my hands. "Baby, baby," she cried. "You keep." As balm for an aching heart she had given me her only valued possession to soothe and comfort me. Moments later Hanna arrived with a small box tied with a blue bow. "Here, use this at the funeral," she said. Before she hobbled away she kissed my cheek. I slowly opened the box and unfolded the tissue paper. Three rows of intricate tatting adorned the edge of the beautiful white handkerchief.

Overwhelmed by these gifts of love, I stepped out into the hall. Then I saw the half-opened door leading to Thelma and Millie's room. I walked across the hall and peeked inside. They were sitting together in their wheel chairs facing the door. They were expecting me. With arms extended towards me I felt their unconditional love. Millie's frail arms circled me while Thelma stroked my hair. I leaned on their love and gave into mourning.

On this day I realized that the sweetest fruits of all, from these precious older ones, were their gifts of love. Old trees still bear fruit.

Epilogue

*T*here is a perfect time of life when the scenes will never again be as clear, the people so real and powerful.

Today I find myself not remembering last evening but reliving tender moments from my past. These portraits, memories of dear and special people, frame my existence and bring truth to my unfinished soul.

I will be eternally grateful to those wonderful, fascinating, and loving people who crossed my path and left part of themselves with me——my mother and father, my nanny, Hattie, Grandmothers Thorpe and Harris, Michael, a stranger, and many more.

And, as I grow to completion, new portraits will be added . . . .